D1607005

Shaping Materials

TWIST IT!

by Tammy Enz

capstone

DISCARDED

SLINGER COMMUNITY LIBRARY

© 2018 Heinemann Raintree
an imprint of Capstone Global Library, LLC
Chicago, Illinois

To contact Capstone Global Library, please call 800-747-4992,
or visit our web site www.capstonepub.com

All rights reserved. No part of this publication may be reproduced or transmitted in any form or by any means, electronic or mechanical, including photocopying, recording, taping, or any information storage and retrieval system, without permission in writing from the publisher.

Edited by Linda Staniford
Designed by Kayla Rossow
Original illustrations © Capstone Global Library Limited 2018
Picture research by Kelli Lageson
Production by Victoria Fitzgerald
Originated by Capstone Global Library Ltd

21 20 19 18 17
10 9 8 7 6 5 4 3 2 1

Library of Congress Cataloging-in-Publication Data
Library of Congress Cataloging-in-Publication Data is available on the Library of Congress website.
ISBN: 978-1-4846-4096-8 (library hardcover)
ISBN: 978-1-4846-4100-2 (paperback)
ISBN: 978-1-4846-4102-6 (eBook PDF)

This book has been officially leveled using the F&P Text Level Gradient™ Leveling System.

Acknowledgments
We would like to thank the following for permission to reproduce photographs: Capstone Studio: Karon Dubke, cover, 1, 8, 9, 12, 13, 14, 15, 18, 19, 22, (bottom left and bottom right); Shutterstock: Africa Studio, 6, alexkich, 17, 22, (middle right), Brent Hofacker, 20, corlaffra, 10, goldenjack, 7, 22, (top right), In Art, back cover, 11, 22, (top left), Janis Smits, 4, Komkrit Noenpoempisut, 21, Maryna Pleshkun, 5, Natasha R. Graham, cover (background), pro500, throughout (background), Tortoon, back cover, 16

Every effort has been made to contact copyright holders of material reproduced in this book. Any omissions will be rectified in subsequent printings if notice is given to the publisher.

All the Internet addresses (URLs) given in this book were valid at the time of going to press. However, due to the dynamic nature of the Internet, some addresses may have changed, or sites may have changed or ceased to exist since publication. While the author and publisher regret any inconvenience this may cause readers, no responsibility for any such changes can be accepted by either the author or the publisher.

Printed and bound in China
PO010438F17

Table of Contents

Some words are shown in bold, **like this**.
You can find out what they mean by looking
in the glossary.

What Twists?

You **twist** something by grabbing its ends. Now turn them opposite ways.

Some materials like string and paper twist easily. Other things are hard to twist. Can you twist a tree branch or a spoon?

Materials that Untwist

Some materials that **twist** easily **untwist**, too. They untwist because they are **elastic**. Twist a piece of ribbon tightly. It untwists when you let go.

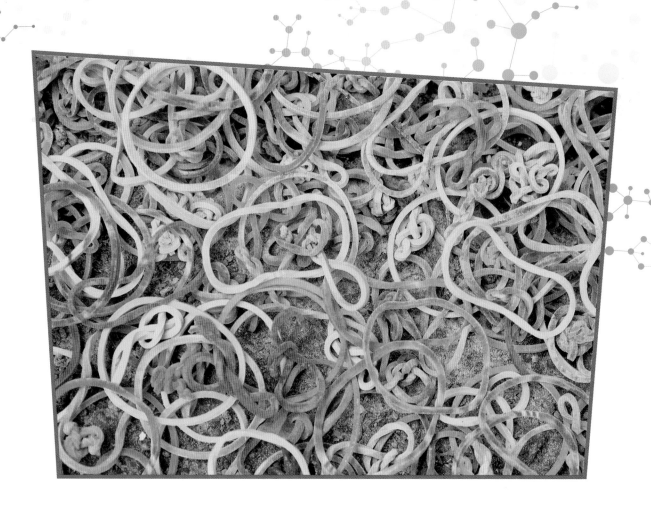

You can twist a rubber band
a lot. It still easily untwists.
A piece of string untwists too.

Project: Bat Mobile

A rubber band **twists** and **untwists** easily. Try it out with this project.

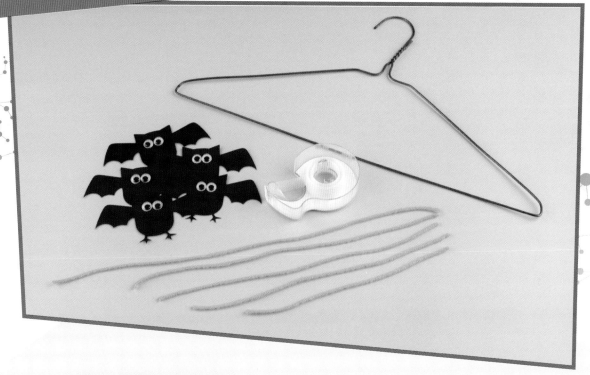

You Will Need:

- 5 small bats cut from black paper
- 5 pieces of string (different lengths)
- Tape
- Wire coat hanger
- Rubber band

What To Do:

1. Tape one end of each string to a bat.
2. Tie the other ends to the bottom of
   the hanger.
3. Slide the hanger hook on the rubber band.
4. Get an adult to help you hang the rubber
   band up. Put it in a place where it has
   space to spin.
5. Twist the rubber band about 20 times.
6. Let go. What happens?

Materials That Twist and Stay

Not all materials that **twist** easily are **elastic**. Wire and threads twist easily. But they usually stay twisted.

Rugs and **fabrics** are made from twisted threads. Chains and wire clothes hangers are made from twisted wire.

Project:
Bubble Wand

There is wire inside pipe cleaners.
You can **twist** it to make a bubble wand.

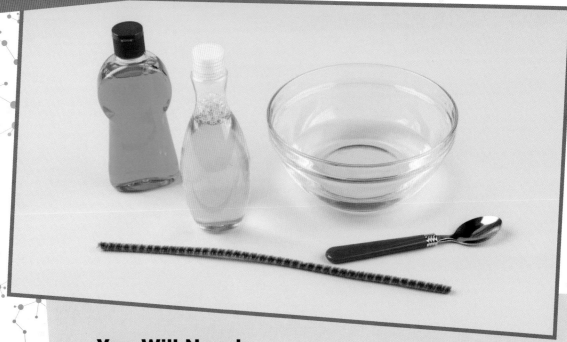

You Will Need:

- Pipe cleaner
- 1 cup (240 mL) water
- 1/4 cup (60 mL) dishwashing liquid
- 1 tablespoon (15 mL) light corn syrup
- Dish and spoon

What To Do:

1. Bend one end of the pipe cleaner into a 1-inch- (3-centimeter-) wide circle. Twist this end 3-4 times around the pipe cleaner.
2. Mix the water, dishwashing liquid, and syrup together.
3. Dip the circle into the mixture. Pull it out. Blow on it to make bubbles.
4. Notice how the wire inside the pipe cleaner holds its new shape.

SLINGER COMMUNITY LIBRARY

Project: Gift Cracker

Wire breaks if **twisted** too much. So does paper. Twist paper carefully to make this project.

You Will Need:

- Cardboard tube
- Sheet of tissue paper (about 18 inches by 18 inches (46 cm x 46 cm))
- Tape
- Several small candies
- A friend

What To Do:

1. Tape one edge of the paper to the tube.
2. Roll the paper around the tube.
   Tape the other edge down.
3. Place the candies inside the tube.
4. Twist each end of the paper carefully to close it.
5. Grab one end. Have a friend grab the other. Pull until the cracker pops open!
6. Share the treats.
7. Notice that the twisted paper holds its shape. But it tears if you twist it too far.

Materials That Twist and Break

Other materials break when **twisted**. Try twisting a cooked noodle.

Twist a flower petal. After a few turns it will break. Things that break easily when twisted are called **fragile**.

Project: Twisted Shells Necklace

Clay is fun and easy to **twist**. But if you twist it too much, what happens? It breaks. Try it out with this project.

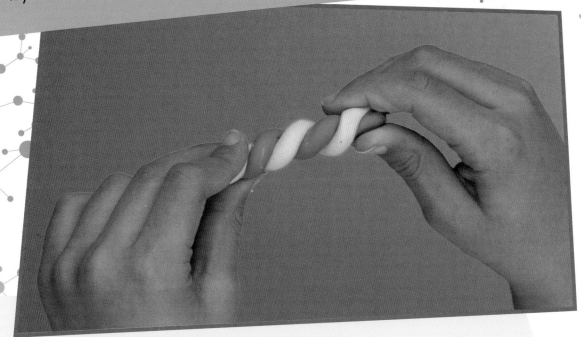

You Will Need:

- 2 different colors of play dough or clay
- Toothpick or cocktail stick (optional)
- Heavy duty thread (optional)

What To Do:

1. Roll each color of clay into
   a 1 inch (2.5 cm) rope.
2. Lay the rolls next to each other.
3. Hold one end of the rolls. Twist off
   a 1/2 inch (1.25 cm) section. Notice how
   easily the clay breaks when it is twisted.
4. Poke a hole through each roll.
   Use the toothpick.
5. Let the shells dry for 2-3 days.
6. Thread the dried shells on the thread.

You Twist It!

Lots of materials can **twist**. Rubber, paper, clay, and metal all act differently when twisted.

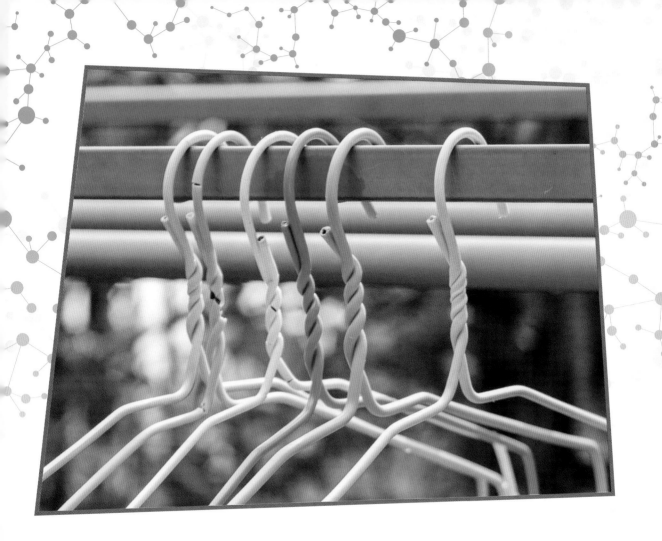

Try out some other things. Find some things that twist and **untwist**. Find some that twist and break. Are there some things that don't twist at all?

Picture Glossary

elastic   able to stretch out and return to its original size and shape

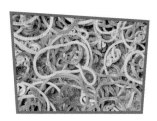

fabric   cloth or a soft material

fragile   easily broken

twist   to turn or wind

untwist   to bring something out of a twisted state

Find Out More

Challoner, Jack. *Hands-On Science: Matter and Materials.* New York, N.Y.: Kingfisher, 2013.

Rompella, Natalie. *Experiments in Material and Matter with Toys and Everyday Stuff.* Mankato, Minn.: Capstone Press, 2015.

Ventura, Marne. *Fun Things to do with Cardboard Tubes.* Mankato. Minn.: Capstone Press, 2015.

Use FactHound to find Internet sites related to this book.

Visit *www.facthound.com*

Just type in 9781484640968 and go!

Super-cool stuff! Check out projects, games and lots more at
www.capstonekids.com

Index

JAN - - 2018